1,003 Great Things to Smile About

1,003 Great Things to Smile About

Copyright © 2004 by Lisa Birnbach, Ann Hodgman, and Patricia Marx.
All rights reserved. Printed in the United States of America. No part of this book
may be used or reproduced in any manner whatsoever without written permission
except in the case of reprints in the context of reviews. For information, write
Andrews McMeel Publishing, an Andrews McMeel Universal company,
4520 Main Street, Kansas City, Missouri 64111.

04 05 06 07 08 BID 10 9 8 7 6 5 4 3 2 1

ISBN: 0-7407-4164-0

Library of Congress Control Number: 2003112473

Book design by Holly Camerlinck

Attention: Schools and Businesses

Andrews McMeel books are available at quantity discounts with bulk purchase
for educational, business, or sales promotional use. For information, please write to:
Special Sales Department, Andrews McMeel Publishing, 4520 Main Street,
Kansas City, Missouri 64111.

1,003
Great Thing
Smile Abou

Lisa Birnbach, Ann Hodgman, Patrici

**Andrews McMeel
Publishing**

Kansas City

1,003 Great Things to Smile About

Smiling uses twenty-six muscles. That beats going to the gym, doesn't it?

The ice cream truck is here!
The ice cream truck is here!

You found your keys!

He asked you to the prom?!

Your old jewelry box
with the dancing ballerina.

The way the sunlight pokes through
the trees after a rain shower.

He *finally* admitted he was wrong.

The doctor gave you *two* lollipops
for not crying.

Congrats! You did everything
on your to-do list. Well, except for
lose ten pounds and learn Italian.

The kids actually put the dishes
into the dishwasher instead of just
stacking them in the sink.

"Memo to Staff: Today's 5:30 P.M.
meeting has been canceled."

Snow day!

Your friend isn't mad at you:
She didn't return your call
because she was out of town.

Your first kiss.

Your dog is always
insanely happy to see you.

The sitter is free tomorrow night.

Your sister will do Thanksgiving
this year.

Friday . . .

The way Play-doh smells.

Finding twenty dollars
in your old jean-jacket pocket.

They say it's going to be sunny
all weekend.

People with pets recover faster
from illnesses.

For no good reason, putting a
AAA sticker on your car makes you
feel a little safer.

You're an adult, so you can buy
as many Snickers bars as you want . . .

. . . **a**nd eat them for breakfast.

Your extra-large threadbare sweatpants.

Pussy willows—the nicest sign of spring.

By the time you read this, some new trend will have replaced reality TV.

There are some great cookie-cutter shapes out there.

Chocolates on your pillow at the hotel.

Scientists are working on miniature grass that won't need as much mowing.

Hybrid cars are coming along nicely.

Celestial Seasonings boxes
are always fun to read.

A rainy day equals a free car wash.

America's favorite Jelly Belly flavor:
Buttered Popcorn.

It feels so cozy after you
punch the snooze button.

They make thongs in large sizes now
(if this is important to you).

Sunless tanning creams really work!

Nowadays you can get a decent
cup of coffee just about anywhere.

Your son remembers your birthday . . .
and doesn't call collect!

Watching kids run under the sprinkler.

Weeds that are prettier
than the grass they spring up in.

Christmas on a Thursday—
a five-day weekend.

Beatrix Potter's books.

Decorative banners on city streets.

Admit it—bathroom humor
is always funny.

It's a beach day!

*T*hose big diamond earrings your best friend wears are really cubic zirconia.

*Y*our son realized he didn't want a motorcycle after all.

*E*ven *you* can figure out how to use a digital camera.

*G*ossiping: the greatest sport on earth.

When you visit Paris,
it's okay to skip the Louvre.

Seeing the Eiffel Tower in person
for the first time.

Even a little exercise
is way better than none.

Champagne, champagne, champagne.

New lipsticks.

Lots of phone messages.

No phone messages.

Life becomes so much easier when you start wearing a bathing suit with a skirt.

Bubble wrap to pop.

70 percent off at Saks Fifth Avenue.

It's only 6:30. Another hour to sleep.

Snowboarding down the mountain
without falling.

Hello Kitty.

It's a girl!

It's a boy!

The guy says your computer didn't crash—he can retrieve the files.

Smiling from Start to Finish

Your first pair of loafers.

Your first pair of high heels.

Your first pair of panty hose.

Your first whopper fish—
on your first fishing trip ever.

Your first time getting up
on water skis.

Your first time staying home
without a baby-sitter.

Your first beard (it looks good
no matter what your parents say).

Your first trip to the outlet mall.

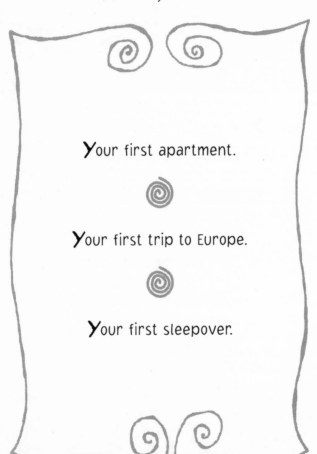

Your first apartment.

Your first trip to Europe.

Your first sleepover.

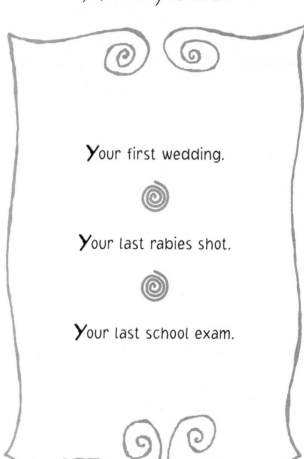

Your first wedding.

Your last rabies shot.

Your last school exam.

Your last mortgage payment.

Your last bite of spinach before
you're allowed dessert.

Your last day of antibiotics.

Your last box unpacked.

Your last thank-you note.

Your last dish of the night
to wash.

Your last hand shaken
in the receiving line.

Your last day before vacation.

Your last day of house arrest.

You can fit into your
favorite pair of jeans again.

TiVo.

The invitation says "No gifts!"

You weren't fired.

The *Sopranos* episodes you missed
are available on videocassette.

Paxil.

You made it from New York to Boston
in less than four hours.

*T*hat worrisome noise in your
car's brakes went away on its own.

*G*o ahead—Super Size the order.
You've had a rough day.

*I*lsa and Rick will always have Paris.

Almost every tough job can be hired out.

Pansies really do
look like cute little faces.

Lilies of the valley really do
look like white coralbells.

The piccolos in
"The Stars and Stripes Forever."

Eggs aren't as bad for you
as they used to say.

Swans may be mean to other birds,
but they sure are beautiful.

Crisp white shirt and blue jeans—
an American classic.

Claritin is available over the counter.

Your checkbook's not lost.
It's under those magazines on
the coffee table.

Washable velvet.

There are no monsters under your bed.
We checked.

A whole dollar! Thank you, Tooth Fairy.

Those noise-canceling headsets
that make airplane trips pass
like a dream.

Fondue sets are back in style.

Blockbuster called. You really did return
those videos you said you'd returned!

Gosh, your kids have good manners.

The coastal highway in your
new Thunderbird.

And did we say the top is down?

You just won $100 in the slots.
(So what if it cost you $150?)

Accutane really clears up acne.

Preparation H really truly reduces
puffiness under the eyes.

Botox really truly amazingly does get rid of migraines.

Netflix provides stamped return envelopes.

Homegrown tomatoes.

Homegrown corn.

One-click shopping.

Rereading *Great Expectations.*

Thank God for the dishwasher.

How did they ever heat up coffee
without a microwave?

And how did they make piecrusts
without food processors?

A photo of Cher from any
stage of her career.

Three-year-olds high-fiving.

George Clooney.

Cary Grant.

Dachshund puppies.

Magazines that devote entire
special issues to celebrity plastic surgery.

*T*elevision makeover shows.

*Y*ou were picked by a cool Secret Santa.

*W*hen your shoes actually match your bag. (And your scarf works with your skirt.)

A clean, nice-smelling taxi . . .

. . . **w**ith a driver who speaks English and knows how to drive safely to your destination.

An old friend works at DreamWorks.

*F*resh-squeezed lemonade.

*T*he *Nutcracker* Christmas tree
magically starting to grow.

"*A* smile cures the wounding of a frown."
(Shakespeare)

Catching the home-run ball
in the stands.

Your spouse surprises you
by picking you up at the airport.

Knowing someone has a crush on you.

Your elegant engraved stationery.

A carton of Chubby Hubby all for you.

Pretending that you hate to watch
the Miss America Pageant.

No one else is using the steam room.

Skinny-dipping in your pool
when the kids are away.

Herb Alpert performing the theme
from *Casino Royale.*

Just remembering Herb Alpert's name.

You spring-cleaned without
killing your back.

Watching the baby wake up, look up, recognize you, and smile.

Sunsets at the beach.

A free slice of chocolate cake at the restaurant on your birthday.

Parents' Visiting Day.

No one else in the elevator.

Finding *The Official Preppy Handbook*
at a yard sale for a dollar.

Your daughter's ballet recital.

Your son's first voice-mail message describing his whole play date.

Children's bathroom wallpaper.

All of Albert Brooks's movies.

*T*he lower school talent show, or
Just because you dress like Avril Lavigne
doesn't mean you sound
like Avril Lavigne.

*L*ast night's two-hour conversation with
your best friend from high school.

*T*he perfect roast chicken.

The sound of your daughter's footsteps
when she tiptoes in the door at 1:33 A.M.

Your student government victory,
undimmed by these many years.

A perfect lanyard.

Reading *Pippi Longstocking*
with your twins.

The day you got into law school.

The day you got out of law school.

New Year's Day brunch.

Mastering the hula hoop.

The first time your husband referred to you as his girlfriend.

When Wayne Newton dedicated a song to you at his show in Las Vegas.

Your child sends a thank-you note
without being told to.

Your friends got on the JumboTron
at the basketball game.

We're number 1!

Little girls in matching dresses.

Sharpie markers come in every
color and width.

Socks with ladybugs on them.

School pictures—before the retakes.

The laundry is folded and put away.

There's always a *Seinfeld* rerun on TV.

You're registered with Do Not Call. Good-bye, telemarketers!

Making the honor roll.

Making the dean's list.

Red mittens on mitten clips.

You won the guess-how-many-gumdrops-are-in-the-jar contest at the library!

Only one more hour until your afternoon nap.

A hamster whose cheeks are stuffed
with sunflower seeds.

A child whose cheeks are stuffed
with grapes.

*T*hose top-of-the-head ponytails
on toddler girls.

Finding a Monopoly house
inside your boot.

Rolling down a hill.

A fresh-raked pile of leaves just waiting
for you to jump into.

Why Is Mona Lisa Smiling?

Leonardo da Vinci is wearing
a Groucho mustache and glasses.

She knows how good she looks
in black.

She knows she's going to be living in Paris.

Il vino.

The art student sketching her in the Louvre is really cute.

This is definitely her last posing job.

The Renaissance is fun.

In her last portrait, she was serious,
and it was a mistake.

Ackkkkkk! This water is *freezing!*

The pictures that Grandma
saved from when you were little.

The prize in the Cracker Jack box.

The whole *jar* of prizes at
the dentist's office.

A fresh jar of Nutella,
Four Weddings and a Funeral on TV,
and no one home but you.

The theater darkens and the
curtain goes up.

Yea! You got a red gumball.

*T*hat lady's stomach made a
funny noise during church.

*Y*our secret love gave you a valentine!

*G*etting home from school on your
birthday and seeing that your mother
put up a huge "It's Great to Be Eight"
banner on your house.

All the magazines in the waiting room
are great ones that you haven't read.

You finished your first 5K race.
So what if you came in second to last?

Your kids cleared the table
without being asked.

Austin Powers.

BabyGap's versions of GapKids clothes.

E-Z Pass.

Finding sea glass on the beach.

*F*lip-flops are back.

"*W*rinkles should merely indicate
where smiles have been."
(Mark Twain)

*E*yeglasses for children are now cute!

A freshly made B.L.T.

Extended-wear and disposable
contact lenses.

Horseradish mashed potatoes in which
you can actually taste the horseradish.

Your collection of *Seventeen*s
dating back to sixth grade.

His collection of *Playboy*s,
dating back to Barbi Benton.

The nail patch the manicurist
talked you into has done the trick.

Mom did all the mending
the last time she visited.

You found your reading glasses
before your family figured out you'd
lost them (again).

Your daughter was a fabulous
Sancho Panza in her middle school play.

You can still find embroidered
(not printed) name tags for your kids.

Computers are getting smaller
and lighter.

The Container Store.

M&M's are now available in
blue, purple, and pink.

Ghirardelli chocolate chips,
unsweetened chocolate, and brownie mix
can be found in most supermarkets.

Compact fluorescent lightbulbs are
undetectable under lampshades.

You didn't have to take your shoes off
in the airport security check.

The guinea pig had babies!

"Free to Good Home:
Ten Adult Guinea Pigs. Some of them
may be pregnant!"

Makeup with SPF 30.

Your twenty-fifth college reunion
was more fun than anyone
has a right to have.

The Andy Williams Christmas special
is on tonight!

At last, panty hose you can wear
with thong-type sandals.

At last, dental floss that doesn't
shred and get stuck between
your molars.

First frost of the year—
no more weeding.

You were planning to cancel the lunch date, but your friend called to cancel first.

You will not be required to do jury duty for another five years.

Hey, the sand in Bermuda really is pink!

You remembered to send a
Father's Day card in advance and
didn't have to FedEx it.

The detour signs actually did
take you back to the right road.

The sty cleared up in time for
your presentation to the board.

Slap! Got that damn mosquito.

Your teenagers invite you to
watch TV with them.

When your hostess asked you to
say grace, she was just kidding.

Free samples.

Buy one, get one free.

He loves you, he loves you not,
he loves you, he loves you not . . .
he loves you!

You got every question on *Jeopardy!* right! (Too bad you weren't actually on the show.)

Winning is nice, even if it's only tic-tac-toe.

Yo-yos.

A box of peanut brittle at work, and
you're the only one who likes it.

Finishing the Sunday crossword puzzle.

Seventy-five cents in the
telephone coin return.

A little salt and club soda,
and the stain is gone.

Finding a brand-new umbrella in the taxi.

For once, you picked the
right checkout line.

All that credit you get for making
homemade bread.

Your daughter is going to help you
clean out your closets.

Anything that's open
twenty-four hours a day.

Your kids like Bob Dylan
as much as you do.

You noticed the "Wet Paint" sign
just in time.

It took three days, but you remembered
the name of Debby's first husband.

*T*hree under par.

*Y*our brand-new iPod.

*S*omeone buys that junky old desk
at your tag sale.

*F*inding a great antique desk
at a tag sale.

Braces off!

After LASIK, your vision is 20-15
for the first time in your life.

Major League baseball.

Lance Armstrong just won the
Tour de France again!

Baby's down for her nap.

Saltwater taffy stores with taffy-pulling
machines in the window.

Dick and Jane and Curious George
stationery.

Pick-your-own raspberry farms.

Running through the sprinkler.

Finding a flawless sixteen-carat sapphire
on the floor of your car. (Well, wouldn't
you smile if this *did* happen?)

Watching someone laugh at
something he's reading.

—**H**ey, wait, he's reading
1,003 Great Things to Smile About!

*T*he first day it's cold enough
to have a fire in the fireplace.

*T*hey keep figuring out ways to
make ultra-premium ice cream even
ultra-premium-er.

*F*our-leaf clovers in the backyard.

The boring couple can't come to your
dinner party, so now you're left
with only the fun people.

No one realized your bake-sale pie
was from a bakery.

When the Wicked Witch
of the West dissolves.

Different states wrangling over who has the best barbecue sauce.

Robins nesting just outside the kitchen window.

You're sick enough to have to stay in bed but not sick enough to feel bad.

The cleaners admit they lost your
coat and are offering you $250 cash
or a $400 credit.

A coffee place opened
in the lobby of your building.

You can put your unwanted old stuff
in boxes, someone will pick it up from
your back door, *and* they'll give you
a tax deduction!

Kiehl's lip balm now comes in
three tints.

A steel watch with diamonds on it
is called a sports watch.

PayPal.

*E*veryone thinks your
cubic zirconia studs are real.

*T*he memory of when you
modeled in college.

*S*ure, your daughter could have modeled,
too, but you wanted her to have a life.

Your kids' palpable delight at
playing with Play-Doh all afternoon.

Your baby-sitter tried to
write a book, too!

"Smile; it's the second-best thing
one can do with one's lips."
(Anonymous)

The rental car's air-conditioning works.

Is it just from this angle,
or does my butt really look smaller?

You surprised your boss
and got the assignment done.

No bruise when you had your blood
taken today.

Your reading glasses prescription
is readily available at the drugstore.

You found the perfect piece for
your friend's penguin collection.

You can still read some of your
old love letters when you're having
a rough day.

A letter from your son at camp
(not a single word is correctly spelled,
but so what?).

Your new phone number
is so easy to remember.

The extension cord reaches.

They accepted your bid.

Hold That Smile!

The camera cuts to you after the announcement that Nicole Kidman, not you, has won the Oscar.

You do a triple-toe loop and land on your rear end during your Olympic figure skating program.

During the whole morning, only one person has come to your booth at the church bazaar.

(And she keeps touching everything but not buying anything.)

(And now she's walking away.)

*T*he plane goes *thrummmp,* and
your eight-year-old asks if
anything's wrong.

*U*h-oh, the waiter is bearing down
on your table with a
lit birthday cake.

The party is so loud you can't hear
a word of the story your friend
is telling you.

You run into an old boyfriend who
describes, in great detail, how
adorable his new baby is.

Seems like the photographer will *never* be done taking the graduation-class photo.

Your great-aunt watches eagerly as you open her present— a white plastic purse.

Whenever you go to Bruce
and Jenny's house, their dog insists
on sitting on your lap.

And Bruce and Jenny insist on
making their children sing a
little good-night song to the
assembled grown-ups.

*T*hat horrible guy at the bar
just sent you a drink.

*A*t your retirement party, one of the
"roasts" is that really mean story
about the time you threw up
on your boss's shoes.

Someone set up your new computer.

Your daughter outgrew those pants
you wanted to throw out.

The dentist says he can save the tooth.

Your broken oven fixed itself.

Over there! The Big Dipper!

Your youngest child outgrows Barney.

Making it all the way down the mountain
without falling.

Yours is better than the one
on *Antiques Roadshow* estimated at
$2,000 to $2,500.

The Christmas shopping is done.

Not one fight during the entire
Thanksgiving vacation.

You found the Afikomen.

Three-day weekend.

The dental hygienist says she's pleased
with what she sees.

The horse you bet on won the race!

Your home is appraised for
a ton of money.

Self-cleaning ovens.

The telephone redial button.

You unwrapped a CD in less than an hour
without swearing.

Your friend canceled. You can stay home
tonight and watch TV.

"They're playing our song."

Diving into the water when it's 102 degrees outside.

A perfect suntan.

A strike the first time you bowl.

Shaq makes a basket in the last second and the Lakers win.

First-row seats at the U.S. Open.

Flamenco dancing.

Finishing your sit-ups for the day.

Your boss keeps praising your work.

Until you pulled out your old photo albums, you'd forgotten how good you looked with bangs.

"You like me. You really like me!"

Kissing on the street corner.

Everybody does love Raymond.

The first time you two held hands.

Whoops! Your flight was overbooked
and you've been bumped . . .
to First Class.

You found your perfect hairdo.

Your daughter got a
fabulous summer job.

Getting a chance to help your mentor.

My cell phone is smaller
than your cell phone.

Sunday night buffets at the club.

The Crayola box of sixty-four crayons with the sharpener in the back.

My prom dress was a size 4???!!!
I used to be a size 4????

You were the first of your friends
to discover: edamame, Club Monaco,
and bluefly.com.

Donald Trump's comb-over.

Telling on your brother.

Seeing your ex
when you're with a partner.

The first time you use your baby
as an excuse to get out of an
unpromising social obligation.

Buying that cashmere sweater on sale
and not telling anyone.

Lying on your Weight Watchers
food diary.

"Everyone smiles in the same language."
(Anonymous)

You had an entire conversation
with a French person
(about the weather, but still . . .).

Smile because you're *not*
on *Candid Camera.*

No morning classes this semester.

The dry cleaners found your white shirt.

Restaurants that give
unlimited iced-tea refills.

Your bangs finally grew out.

The first time your parents let you
stay alone without a baby-sitter.

A bowl full of caviar.

He asked you out for New Year's Eve!

A bicycle built for two.

Sounds That Bring a Smile

Mourning doves in the morning.

The old *Tonight Show (Starring Johnny Carson)* theme music.

The crashing of the surf.

The wind howling outside
when you're snug in bed.

Your son practicing for his
bar mitzvah when he doesn't know
you're listening.

*Y*our preschool daughter singing
"Happy Birthday" to herself
in bed at night.

*T*he sound of your bath filling.

*T*he clang of the busy cash register
at your own garage sale.

*T*he whoosh of the snow
as you execute a perfect ski turn.

*T*he first popping kernel of popcorn.

*T*he last car pulling out of
your driveway as the
final guests leave.

*T*he hush as you turn on
the Christmas tree lights for the
first time this year.

*T*he end-of-the-period bell
telling you chemistry class
is finally over.

A cat purring.

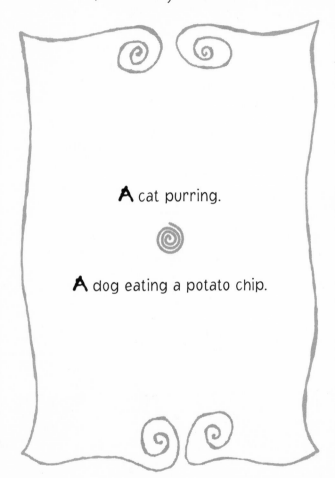

A dog eating a potato chip.

You made the cheerleading squad.

No more morning sickness.

Acing your serve.

$200 round-trip New York–London.

Walking on stilts.

Blowing out all the birthday candles
on your cake.

You don't pick up when he calls.
Thank you, caller ID.

Pogo sticks.

Your horoscope says that you will be
unimaginably happy tomorrow.

Checkmate.

Room service.

Sunday comics.

Online Scrabble at 3:00 A.M.

The guy with spinach in his teeth the whole time he was chairing the meeting.

You were the only person at the party sensible enough not to waste time on a pedicure.

(You scheduled a pedicure as soon as you got home from the party.)

You overheard the nurse saying
you had the best attitude of any
patient on the floor.

Being the first to hear juicy new gossip.

A stroller where the baby faces you.

Toothpaste is excellent for minimizing blemishes.

By the time you have the guts to have plastic surgery, it'll be even better than it is today.

The plastic surgeon says you aren't ready for an eye lift.

The deer fence seems to be working.

You and your daughter can wear
the same clogs.

The Senegalese copy of your Louis
Vuitton bag seems to fool everyone.

If you hadn't tried the free sample at the gourmet store, you would have no idea that you love ginger sesame salad dressing.

The Sunday Style section of the *New York Times*.

Your hair is long enough to put in a ponytail.

A stash of comic books.

A care package of Grandma's brownies.

Mmmm, those candles smell
like a garden.

Biking down the boardwalk
in Atlantic City.

Buying Boardwalk in Monopoly.

Did you ever gunnel on a canoe?

Any of the eight world wonders.

A helicopter ride.

There's only one person ahead of you in line at the post office.

Pigs in a blanket.

Christmas carols, up to a point.

When the bride and the groom kiss.

Your six-year-old still wants
to cuddle with you.

Band-Aids that are contoured
to fit any finger.

Homemade guacamole.

Lemon poppy-seed muffins.

A perfect day for seersucker.

Your bifocals lenses really are invisible.

The way the first slice of pizza you take out of the box drips mozzarella.

Your old college roommate found you
through the Internet.

Recognizing famous voices like
Lauren Bacall's, Gene Hackman's, or
James Earl Jones's in TV commercials.

You got rid of your pimple
before anyone saw it.

Rogaine grows eyebrows!

*Y*ou were rooting for Miss Idaho
and she won!

*S*etting out on a cross-country trip.

*W*ater has no calories.

*T*he newspaper delivered to your door
every morning.

Watching *Singin' in the Rain* on TV
at 2:00 A.M.

Moist towelettes.

Help yourself to butter and cream
on the Atkins diet.

Clean sheets.

A great salsa partner.

A hole in one!

The new house came with
a nice bottle of wine
chilling in the fridge.

That first "Mama" from your baby.

The Fig Newtons were still moist.

When you find your copy of
L'Etranger from eleventh-grade
French class, and it has the note
on which you practiced your
married name (to the boy you can
no longer remember exactly).

Still-warm chocolate pudding.

The tummy tuck was worth it.

At your twentieth college reunion,
you looked good . . .

. . . and your old roommate looked old.

And your old boyfriend
had much less hair on his head
(although plenty in his ears).

Today is the birthday of your
best friend from sixth grade.
And you still remember it.

Benecol tastes okay on a baked potato.

The generosity of a wrap skirt.

Smiling Through the Ages

1 day old: That's not really a smile. It's just gas.

1 week old: Still just gas.

2 weeks old: Probably just a reflex.

4 weeks old: Okay, a real smile!
Who cares that the cause was
the picture of the baby
on the diaper box?

6 weeks old: At last,
a real smile because the baby
recognizes Mommy.

3 months old: The sight of an open bar (aka Mommy's boob).

6 months old: I can sort of sit up!

8 months old: I can sort of crawl (backward)!

1 year old: Ah, a bookshelf full of nice books for me to pull out onto the floor.

18 months old: Ah, a nice DVD player that I can feed pennies into and break.

2 years old (male): A fire truck screaming on its way to a major catastrophe.

2 years old (female):
Sandals with Barbie on them.

3 years old: The word *bottom*.

4 years old: The word *doody*.

5 years old: The word *butt.*

6 years old: The word *underpants.*

7 years old: The word *bra.*

8 years old: EXamine Your Zipper!

9 years old: Michael tried to kiss Caitlyn!

10 years old: Your hair looks almost exactly like Hilary Duff's!

11 years old: Time for a (training) bra!

12 years old: Got asked to dance!

13 years old: Received twenty silver necklaces for your bat mitzvah!

14 years old: Parents admitted you're too big for them to physically force you to take piano anymore.

15 years old: Parents agree you have too much homework to have to go to church anymore.

16 years old: Excellent fake ID.

17 years old: Another excellent fake ID—this one from a different state.

18 years old: Finally old enough to forget to vote.

21 years old: Legal at last.

26 years old: Your first non-Goodwill sofa.

30 years old: People in their forties laugh when they hear you say you're getting old.

37 years old: You can pass for 30.

39 years old: You can pass for 33.

40 years old: You can pass for 39.

43 years old: You can pass for 43.

50 years old: Everyone says this is when the fun *really* starts.

55 years old: Cheeseburger and fries again. Thank you, Lipitor.

58 years old: You are mistaken for a parent at Take Your Grandparent to School Day.

65 years old: Wow. A movie ticket for five dollars with your senior citizen card.

67 years old: Still playing in a weekly tennis game.

71 years old: no chance of having a midlife crisis now.

72 years old: What a lively singles scene at your fiftieth reunion.

88 years old: Finally. Time to read *War and Peace*.

90 years old: You'll never have to play another game of Duck, Duck, Goose.

Grown-up goodie bags with goodies
you actually like!

Impressing your kids when you know
the lyrics to songs on the radio.

(Then again, you were listening
to Lite-FM.)

Aspirin usually gets rid of
your headache . . .

. . . and it can help get rid of a
heart attack as well.

The stains did come out!

Eyebrow shaping is now an art form.

You're getting a massage tomorrow.
From Lars.

A warm, fluffy towel straight
from the dryer.

Blueberries are effective as antioxidants.

You actually drank the recommended
sixty-four ounces of water today!

You were elected to Phi Beta Kappa.

Reruns of *Gilligan's Island.*

"*J*udy in Disguise with Glasses."

*R*emembering the power shortage
you created at sleepaway camp/boarding
school/your college dorm when
every girl plugged in her blow dryer
at the same time.

*H*earing "My Sharona" on the radio.

After walking fifteen blocks
in your new mules, your feet
don't hurt *that* much.

Look, Ma! No cavities!

An agent called to say he thinks
you're talented.

Coffee with half-and-half.

Saturday Night Live—the early years.

You managed to re-gift those ugly tumblers!

Cash refunds instead of merchandise credits.

The first gin and tonic of the summer.

Lilac season.

Your kids ask for seconds.

"Did you go on vacation? You look so refreshed."

The way your husband beams at you.

After you've spent the day online, your nail polish hasn't chipped.

Finding those shoes on sale.

The opening theme to *Sex and the City.*

Non-greasy fried chicken.

Sauerkraut on hot dogs at
baseball games.

The opening page of
Pride and Prejudice.

"I am Eloise. I am six."

Getting to toss your tassel
at graduation.

Your new issue of *People* just arrived.

A business trip. To Paris.

Smile Facts

The first known smiley face
was drawn in 1963 by Harvey Ball,
graphic artist who was hired by the
State Mutual insurance company,
whose promotional director
wanted a symbol for their
morale-boosting campaign.

The smiley face craze was started
in 1971 by Bernard and Murray Spain,
who lived in Philadelphia and
sold novelty items.

Humans are the only creatures
who laugh.

*T*he average adult laughs
seventeen times a day.

*W*omen laugh more loudly among
male strangers, but men laugh
the most among their friends.

Scientists still don't know why
you can't tickle yourself.

Researchers estimate that laughing
a hundred times is equal to
ten minutes on the rowing machine
or fifteen minutes on an
exercise bike.

Some scientists believe the first laughter was an expression of shared relief at the passing of danger.

A smile can be seen from thirty-three feet away.

If you force yourself to smile when you aren't in a good mood, you will become happier.

There're still a couple of pictures
in your camera.

An armful of bangles.

The new puppy peed on the newspaper.

The trainer at the health club
looks like a young Sean Connery.

You had an umbrella in the
backseat after all.

Cutting down on carbs really works.

The movie box office doesn't believe
you are a senior citizen.

Your night in the Lincoln Bedroom.

Bringing Up Baby.

Is there anything chic-er
than your mom's old Pucci?

Linguine alla pesto.

Sitting around with old friends, singing old commercial jingles.

Your hair colorist just returned from vacation.

Next week at this time,
you'll be at the spa.

What you thought sushi would taste like
before you ever tried it.

Your bra size changed.

(**F**or the better.)

A drawer full of gift certificates . . .
for when you need them.

Reading to your daughter's
kindergarten class.

Chaperoning your son's
sixth-grade dance.

Seeing your byline for the
very first time.

Your teeth after a cleaning
at the dentist's.

When the pediatrician says your child
doesn't need any shots today.

*F*irst snowman of the year
(made from one inch of slush).

*S*omeone returned the cell phone
you left in the taxi.

*S*pell-check.

That stock went up twelve points!

Your cholesterol went down
forty points!

You've reached thirty thousand
frequent-flier miles.

Hoop earrings never went out of style.

Falling in love with a book and
finding out it's the first of a series.

Getting a thick envelope
from your first-choice college.

"*D*o you want to go steady?"

*T*he memory of your uncle gatoring
at a family wedding.

*T*he Grand Canyon.

*T*he last time you went to a
drive-in movie.

*Y*our toddler tells everyone that your
husband snores.

"*A* smile is a light in the window of the
soul indicating that the heart is at home."
(Anonymous)

Sesame Street is still on the air.

*H*arvey Fierstein in *Hairspray.*

*Y*our four-year-old is scared of clowns but loves roller coasters.

You were the first one in your town
to get a French manicure.

Your youngest child's passport photo—
more of your hand than her face.

You won the office Oscars pool.

Remembering the night you found out
what happens when you mix liquors
in your stomach.

When your mom tried to copy
Farrah Fawcett's hairdo.

Your new eye doctor is *cute*.

The first ski weekend of the year.

Prada, half off.

There's no such thing as bad macaroni and cheese.

Paying by credit card feels like
getting things for free.

The first time you feel
your baby kicking.

Your grandma's charm bracelet.

*J*ust when you thought you'd have to parallel-park, the car in front of the space pulls out.

*T*he smell of suntan lotion during the dead of winter.

A whole day with nothing on your schedule.

Freshly polished toenails.

Realizing those
upper-arm exercises *worked*.

Listening to your book on tape
even after you've parked.

Fresh corn on the cob with melted butter.

The salad bar has artichokes and avocados.

The joke was so filthy you could barely tell it.

The Most Smile-Worthy Inventions

*J*ust when you can't
carry another log . . . the wheel!

*I*ndoor plumbing.

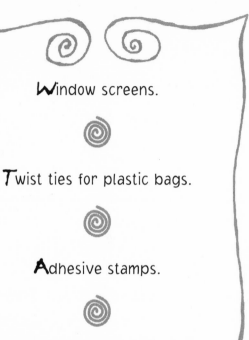

Window screens.

Twist ties for plastic bags.

Adhesive stamps.

Kleenex. (Lotion-impregnated tissues
are the icing on the cake.)

*T*oilet paper. (Quilted toilet paper is gilding the lily.)

*L*uggage on wheels.

*I*nvisible fencing for dogs.

*E*pidurals.

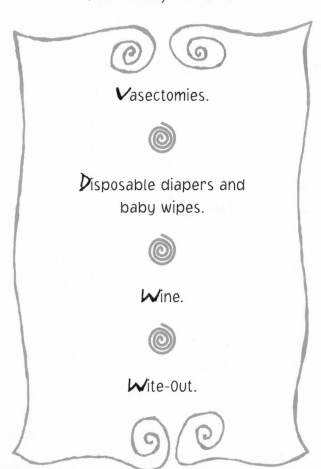

Vasectomies.

Disposable diapers and
baby wipes.

Wine.

Wite-Out.

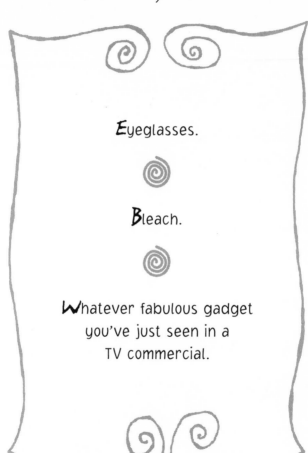

*E*yeglasses.

*B*leach.

*W*hatever fabulous gadget
you've just seen in a
TV commercial.

Fireworks on July Fourth.

How blond your hair got last August.

False alarm—the baby doesn't have a poopy diaper after all.

The time your brother spat his food out at the table because he was laughing so hard.

Your son's face at his bar mitzvah.

The dog is on the table eating the pizza!

Someone's going to win the Powerball lottery. It might as well be you.

You're not too old to wear suede pants.

"You can put the money in the parking meter this time."

Aren't you glad you remember
how to knit?

When you're pregnant, you can finally
eat your own whole dessert.

Sue Grafton isn't done with
the alphabet yet.

Finding an old photograph
of your dad in uniform.

Sorbet is better than sherbet.

You've got mail!

The secret language you share
with your twin.

*Y*our date wore a leisure suit
to your senior prom.

*T*hat vintage watch you got
for a song on eBay.

*V*ideos of you and your brother
singing "The Hokey Pokey."

*T*ankinis let mature women wear
two-piece bathing suits.

Your children when they have lost
their front teeth.

Two-hour Boggle marathons.

Home: 7. Away: 4.

You found a nice, clean new copy of
InStyle in your seat pocket on the plane.

Remember in fourth grade when
you went to the farm and one of the cows
started peeing in front of everyone?

Remember the time the iguana
got out of its tank and ran up
the Christmas tree?

. . . And Dad had to trap it
in a shopping bag?

Collecting free samples in
hotel bathrooms. (Except for the
mouthwash and the little sewing kit
and the shower cap and the
shoeshine cloth.)

You finally got moss to grow
on your flowerpots.

Thank heaven—you won't need a
root canal after all.

*T*he special presents Mommy
gave you on long car trips.

*N*othing feels better than
tweezing out that one particular hair.

*Y*ou're the only one in the family
who likes black jelly beans.

*F*or once there's plenty of ice
in the freezer.

Pictionary—the greatest game ever.

Finding that fan letter you were too scared to send to the Monkees twenty-five (wait—thirty-five!) years ago.

Oh, here's a bag of chocolate chips. Now you don't have to go to the store.

It won't be your turn to drive the car
pool for a long, long time.

"Go in peace to love and serve the Lord."
(Translation: Now you can go home
and read the Sunday *Times.*)

"We won't file charges."

"**T**his won't show up on
your permanent record."

"**O**kay, I'll let you go without
a ticket this time."

Fred Astaire dancing . . .

. . . **or** just walking.

Think of all the money you saved
by not buying every single item
on the infomercials.

Pulling into the driveway after
a two-week vacation to discover . . .
the house has not burned down!

Flexible straws.

Smells to Smile About

Your first girlfriend's perfume.

Freshly mown grass.

Bread in the oven.

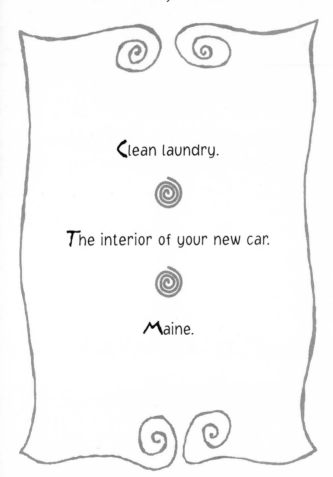

Clean laundry.

The interior of your new car.

Maine.

Christmas cookies.

Babies, post-bath.

Your clean house—
cleaned by someone else.

*M*imeographed copies (if you remember what those were).

L'Occitane lavender hand cream.

*E*verything, once you've quit smoking.

The sound of a summer rainstorm
on your roof.

Watching your best friend (age fifty)
at her first tap recital.

When Dad gets so mad that he
shouts out your brother's name
instead of yours.

Your medical insurance will be
extended another six months.

Your amniocentesis was fine.

Your mother found another four yards
of that discontinued chintz, so you
can repair that old loveseat after all.

*I*t's sidewalk sale time!

*T*hey're giving you a decent per diem.

*Y*our partner's promotion includes
a new leased car.

*F*inders keepers, losers weepers.

Blondes do have more fun, you know.

You can be blond too, you know.

Invisalign braces.

Researchers at Harvard kept tabs on 1,300 healthy men for ten years. At the end of the study, they found that individuals with the most positive attitudes at the start of the trial were half as likely to have experienced heart problems as those with more negative attitudes.

Your daughter is the right amount of homesick. Any more, she'd hate camp; any less, you'd feel unloved.

You made the 5:44!

Your son loves the Doors.

Your favorite niece won a Pulitzer.

Your black sheep nephew
won a Grammy.

*T*he shoe fits.

*I*t's a cyst, not a tumor.

"*S*miles are the language of love."
(David Hare)

"*S*ide out and rotate!
Our team is really great!"

Your partner is taller than you
even when you wear your new
dressy sandals.

You just realized that you know
all the lyrics to Herman's Hermits'
"I'm Henry the VIII I Am."

You made all your callbacks.

Someone referred to you as a girl.

Your insurance does cover
acupuncture, after all.

The new color vocabulary:
windsong, lichen, cloud, berry.

She got a 790 on her verbal SATs!

My son, the doctor.

You're renting a Vespa on your
upcoming vacation.

Your old college is now "hot."

Peppermint-stick ice cream.

Your straight hair is in.

*T*hey really honored the
lifetime warranty!

*Y*ou found your passport!

*S*mile, and the world smiles with you.

*Y*ou really like your son's fiancée.

You actually got great gifts
this birthday.

You rediscover Fresca.

Margaritas!

High-speed Internet.

*J*ust when you thought you were finished with the Easter candy hunt, you discover a treasure trove behind the piano.

*S*unday night on HBO.

*T*here hasn't been an ice age for a long time.

*T*here are very few
poisonous snakes in America.

*F*luoridated water has drastically
cut down the number of cavities.

Anything with coconut.

You found a first-edition copy of
The Story of Dr. Dolittle.

Your seven-year-old *likes*
her tie shoes.

A bra that fits well.

Your kids all love to read.

"He's a chip off the old block."

Your husband thinks you look better
without makeup.

At the bathing suit department, the salesgirl sent you to the bikini section.

Cars with seat heaters . . .

. . . **W**hich feel great when you get that lower back pain.

All the Christmas presents to relatives
have been mailed.

The pastor lost his place big-time
during the sermon.

Seeing that picture of you and your
boyfriend during the disco era.

A blind date that works out.

The smell of Bain de Soleil.

A beautifully framed antique sampler.

Lines That Make Us Smile

"The children are asleep."

"Will you marry me?"

"Score!"

"*I* just heard we're getting *great* bonuses this year."

"**A**nd the award goes to [your name here]."

"**H**ave you lost weight?"

"This one's on me."

"Does anyone want seconds?"

"Can I trust you with this gossip?"

"Did anyone ever tell you that you look just like Prince William?"

"That ball is outa here!"

"The receipt's in the bag
if you want to return it."

"Say cheese!"

"This is my boyfriend."

"This is my girlfriend."

Your college-age son actually
gave you a hug.

*F*inishing the war stories in your newsmagazine and moving on to the gossip section.

*L*ook! Fox cubs in the yard!

*L*ook! An arrowhead!

You found your favorite baking dish in the church kitchen—you must have forgotten it after the last potluck.

Finally you got that seed out from under your bridgework.

Your aunt left you the antique china doll in her will.

You manage to get through a whole ladies' lunch without having to discuss the dangerous topic of who the next president of the United States should be.

The snowdrops are in bloom by your back door.

You've done a good deed without telling anyone.

S'mores.

You were afraid that wave was going to knock you over, but you're still standing.

A kitten really playing with a ball of yarn.

You ate your way through the cruise without gaining an ounce.

Your doctor says you'd better avoid
exercise for the next couple of weeks . . .

. . . and he also thinks you should
try to gain a couple of pounds.

The guy who mows your lawn
got there just before it rained.

You find the last chocolate-covered
caramel in the box.
(It was hidden under a Brazil nut.)

The traffic jam breaks up after a mile.
(It was just someone with a flat tire.)

Discovering that the mass e-mail
about the virus is a hoax.

The beach is about to close
for the night. Go ahead and walk all
over that abandoned sand castle.

Peanuts is still in newspapers,
even though Charles Schulz died
several years ago.

*Y*ou forgot to ask for a no-fat latte,
so they made you one with whole milk.
Oh, well!

Anti-Smiles

Friday night traffic on the
Long Island Expressway.

Childproof medicine containers.

Your passport photo.

"Mommy, I stepped in dog doo!"

Telemarketers selling
accidental death insurance.

Rain on Memorial Day.

"In tonight's performance, the part of Blanche, usually played by Julia Roberts, will be played by Mabel O'Nobody."

"Fatal System Error."

Whoops, red wine on your new dress.

$1,400 vet bill for IV drip
in pet turtle's leg.

"**M**om, John flushed his Batman
down the toilet and now the toilet is
making a funny sound and there's
water all over the floor."

Well-dressed young people standing at the front door, holding pamphlets and smiling.

"Say cheese!"

You got to the movie in time
to see all the previews.

You got to the movie just late enough
to miss all the previews.

Telling a friend that a particularly
shocking piece of gossip isn't true.

At last that splinter is out!

Your antivirus software detected
and quarantined a virus.

"If you haven't seen your wife smile
at a traffic cop, you haven't seen
her smile her prettiest."
(Kin Hubbard)

Bubonic plague is not a realistic cause for concern.

Nor is a return of the Ice Age.

Or an attack by killer bunnies.

Or being lowered into a vat
of boiling oil by the Joker.

New running shoes.

Winning a big stuffed animal
at the fair.

The closet organizer was
worth the money.

How satisfying to have your books
in alphabetical order.

The ticket stub to the movie you
went to on your first date.

After all these years,
your watch still keeps time.

Volume control on phones.

Plasma TV makes even infomercials
look terrific.

A lifetime supply of anything.

Figuring out who killed the victim
before the end of the mystery.

Laminated anything.

Your roses are blooming
despite the frost.

Waking up to the smell of bacon
cooking on a Sunday morning.

Wearing fake wax lips
to a formal dinner.

Your accountant got everything right
on your taxes this year.

You have to pretend to be shocked,
but it's always funny when a two-year-old
belts out his first curse word.

The smoke detector went off only
because it needed a new battery.

The baby's finally gotten over
her stranger anxiety. You can relax
when people say hi to her.

You don't have to carve
the leg of lamb after all.

Pushpins and thumbtacks come in
such cute shapes and colors these days.

Your children's adorable art projects
all magneted to the fridge.

Now that the kids have moved out,
you can finally take down all their
dusty art projects from the fridge.

*T*he chairlift broke down,
so you can go get hot chocolate
with a clear conscience.

*P*hew—it's not a cop car parked
in that speed-trap spot.

. . . *O*h, no, it *is* a cop car, but the
trooper is stopping the car behind you.

*T*he humiliation you just experienced
will make a funny story someday.

There's enough new snow to be pretty but not enough to have to shovel.

The sonogram shows twins!

Wait—it's triplets!

Thank you, Lord—it's just twins!

You've just cleaned your oven,
so now you can wait another
four years to do it again.

The penny you received
in change is rare and valuable.

Guilty Smiles

Guy who broke your heart
ten years ago . . .
three times divorced.

High school chemistry teacher
who gave you an F . . . now sells
Amway on the phone.

Kid you baby-sat for until he
told his parents you stole (untrue) . . .
in jail for grand larceny.

Girl who got all the best parts
in the high school plays . . . now does
local commercials for a
secondhand car company.

Mom who picked on you about every little thing . . . now paying for your therapy.

Woman who campaigned for her daughter's book being bumped to the top of the book club waiting list . . . just heard that her best friend lost *her* spot on the waiting list as a result.

Daughter who went into a rage
when you said her best friend
was "trouble" . . . now prays each
night that her best friend
will move away.

Snotty cheerleader who wouldn't
give you the time of day . . .
now weighs 350 pounds.

Neighbor who called the police because your music was "raucous" . . . indicted for money laundering.

Obnoxious man who worked in cubicle next to yours . . . fired for playing computer games.

Show-off bodybuilder at gym . . . has rotator cuff damage.

Car with bumper sticker that says,
MY KID IS AN HONOR STUDENT AT BHS . . .
just got rear-ended.

Boss who fired you . . .
convicted in
sexual harassment case.

You rode the Thrill Dragster
roller coaster and lived to tell the tale.

Finally, you remember your password.

Your plane landed.

The baby-sitter says the kids were
no trouble at all.

You're not the only one who didn't understand the movie.

Your new jacket matches your old skirt.

You got the trash barrels out thirty seconds before the garbage collectors arrived.

"If you're not using your smile, you're like a man with a million dollars in the bank and no checkbook."
(Les Giblin)

A box of nice hand-me-downs for your newborn.

Giving a box of hand-me-downs to a friend for her newborn.

The restaurant can seat you now.

You get a table overlooking the water.

Your houseguests are going home
a day early.

Self-addressed envelopes.

Remember invisible ink?

Non-greasy sunblock.

You got the big end of the wishbone.

Waking up and finding your
little girl in bed with you.

How versatile are taupe pumps!

You overhear a teenager
praising your tennis serve.

Your kids are playing
nicely together even though
you haven't told them to.

The way your four-year-old mispronounces the word *dwarf* when you read *Snow White.*

The fact that you let him say "dorf" until he was seven.

The baby's tiny toes.

Grammy's weeping willow tree
is still going strong.

Your husband's sister isn't *that* bad.

Your boyfriend tells you you're sexier
than Sarah Jessica Parker.

*T*hat tarnished metal watch
at the junk store turned out to be
a genuine Rolex.

*H*e didn't snore last night.

*Y*our kids seem to like
your college roommate's kids
when you get together.

"Smile, damn it. Smile."
(Dame Sybil Hathaway)

Your alma mater has invited you
back to give a speech.

Your toddler cooperated today when
you had to zip him into his snowsuit.

Your daughter didn't cry during her haircut. Of course, she was sitting on the blue horsie this time.

It looks like at least half that weight is staying off.

A newsy, warm letter (in an envelope) from a pal.

*T*he Brandenburg Concertos during
your morning commute.

*Y*our ancestors seem to have had
their own tartan.

*J*ust enough Advil in your purse
to nail this headache.

In 2004 there's no reason
to still have wrinkles.

Funny—you never realized how
small your old house was until you
moved into a much bigger one.

You are introduced as "my honey."

Falling in love with a new scent.

Your colleagues have bestowed
a cute nickname on you.

At the wedding reception you
parked yourself by the caviar.

"You are my sunshine . . ."

You've got a good connection at your child's first-choice college.

You smell your dad's aftershave before you see him.

A really impressive politician.

Your eight-year-old actually asks you
to cut her nails.

A new watch strap for your
old wristwatch.

You buckled down and cleaned out
the garage.

Your children's friends seem to like you.

Or at least they appreciate the bowl of Poppycock you keep in the den.

Taking your grown daughters to a spa with you for your birthday.

Now you can admit it:
You hate Walt Disney.

At forty-two years old,
you discover you love sailing!

You never knew you'd like
Indian food so much.

Realizing you can go for a swim
after dinner.

Realizing no one can force you
to go for a swim if the water's cold.

A summer storm through the
screened-in porch.

The gym bathrooms have nicer
body lotion than the stuff
you use at home.

He smiled back.

Hot chocolate made with milk,
not water.

A 50 percent off sale at the pro shop.

Compliments on your new lipstick color.

An unbelievably pretentious class note in the alumni magazine from the most pretentious member of your class.

Corny but True Smiles

Autumn in New England.

Snow globes.

Dew on a spiderweb.

Look, a rainbow!

"There's no place like home.
There's no place like home."

Chestnuts roasting on
an open fire.

Catching snowflakes
on your tongue.

A kite flying through the sky.

Baby took his first step!

Chocolates on Valentine's Day.

Finding a four-leaf clover.

An ocean breeze.

Pussy willows.

A nice deep bubble bath.

The book you've been looking for
is available used online for $2.17—
okay, plus three bucks shipping.

Your fortune cookie says
you will live a long and happy life
and own a summer house.

Your son got the male lead
in the play at camp.

The prettiest girl at camp
got the female colead.

"If you can smile when things go wrong,
you have someone in mind to blame."
(Anonymous)

The choir director asked you to do
a solo in church next week.

You did an excellent job of arranging
the flowers, if you do say so yourself.

You found (and threw away) the
source of that horrible mildewy smell
in the closet.

Look! There's Brad Pitt filling up
his car with super unleaded!

Your guests didn't leave until 1:00 A.M.,
so it must have been a good party.

Finding a perfect seashell at the beach.

Your son decides he doesn't
want an ant farm after all.

*T*he penguins at the zoo.

*Y*ou asked the waiter for rare, and he brought you rare.

*Y*ou asked the waiter for no fat, and he brought your fish covered with melted butter. No sense in bothering him about it . . .

What were the chances that you
would find a rug exactly eleven feet
by two feet, seven inches?

"Start off every day with
a simple smile and get it over with."
(W. C. Fields)

Thank God a friend warned you
they were planning a surprise party
for your thirtieth.

You just had an Aha! moment
while reading the map.

You turned on the radio just in time
for *Prairie Home Companion*.

Leftover cookie batter in the bowl.

Discovering a carousel you
never knew about.

You can still touch your toes.

"I love you."